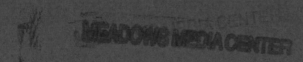

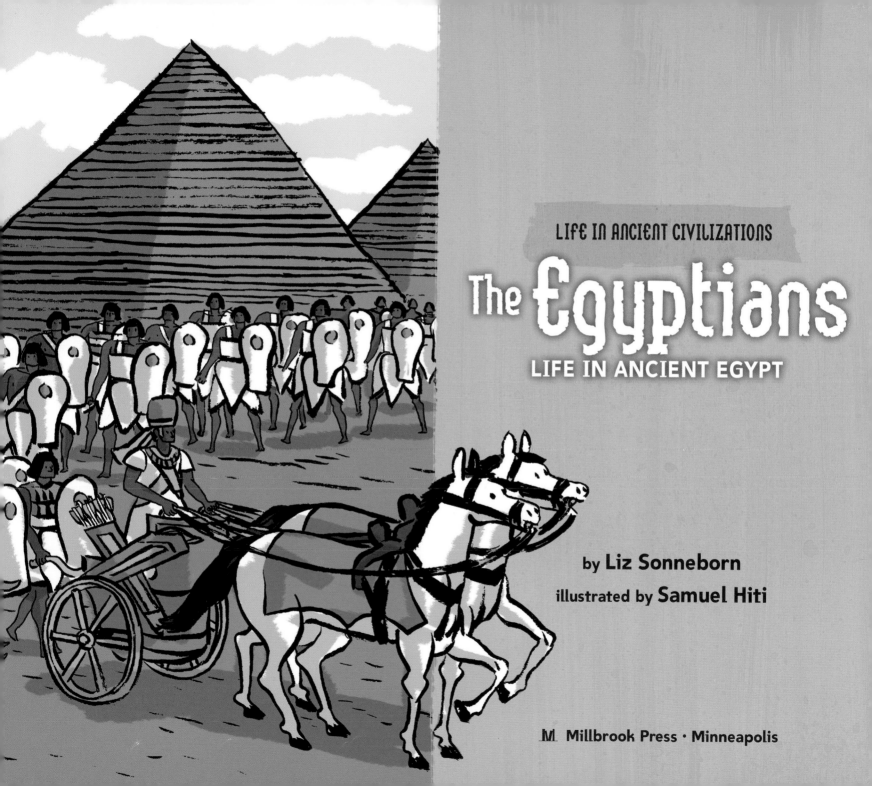

LIFE IN ANCIENT CIVILIZATIONS

The Egyptians
LIFE IN ANCIENT EGYPT

by **Liz Sonneborn**

illustrated by **Samuel Hiti**

M Millbrook Press · Minneapolis

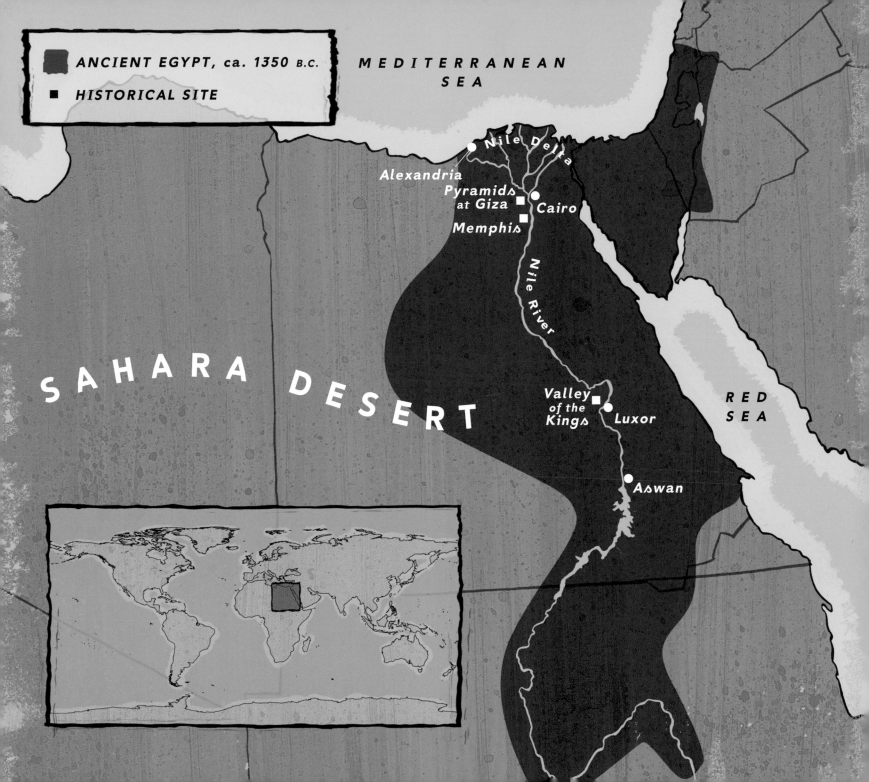

ANCIENT EGYPT, ca. 1350 B.C.

■ HISTORICAL SITE

MEDITERRANEAN SEA

Nile Delta

Alexandria

Pyramids at Giza

Memphis

Cairo

Nile River

SAHARA DESERT

Valley of the Kings

Luxor

RED SEA

Aswan

Introduction

The ancient Egyptians were fascinating people. Long ago, they lived in northeastern Africa. There, beginning in about 3100 B.C., they created a mighty civilization.

Powerful kings called pharaohs ruled ancient Egypt. Under the pharaohs, Egyptians built glorious cities and buildings. They are best known for one type of building—the pyramid. They are also famous for their picture-writing system. It is called hieroglyphics.

The Nile River ran through the Egyptians' land. It provided them with water. It also allowed them to grow food in a very hot, dry climate. They owed their very lives to this river.

CHAPTER ONE
Egyptian Life

Egyptians lived in cities and villages close to the Nile. Each year, summer rain made the river overflow. The rushing water left behind rich soil. Crops grew well there during other seasons. Egyptian farmers planted vegetables, including lettuce, cucumbers, and peas. They also grew fruit trees.

Grains were important crops as well. Egyptians used wheat to make bread, their favorite food.

The waters of the Nile attracted many types of fish and birds. Egyptians often feasted on perch, catfish, or duck.

Rich people ate beef. But meat was expensive. Most Egyptians ate meat only on special days.

Egyptians believed the tears of the goddess Isis made the Nile overflow each year. They celebrated the flood with a festival called the Night of the Drop.

Ordinary Egyptians lived in small, plain houses made from mud bricks. Their clothing was also plain. Women made it from linen. They wove this white cloth with thread made from the flax plant. Men wore a type of skirt. Women wore dresses. Children often didn't wear any clothes at all.

Egyptians dressed up their simple clothing with beautiful jewelry. They wore earrings, bracelets, rings, and necklaces decorated with colorful stones.

Both men and women wore perfume. They also used oil to keep their skin soft in the hot desert air.

This necklace was found in a pharaoh's tomb. It is made of gold and gemstones.

Egyptian men and women wore green and black eye makeup. The makeup made their eyes look bigger.

9

Egyptians belonged to different social classes. The lowest included slaves and servants. Next were workers, such as farmers, craftsmen, and soldiers. Above them were skilled professionals, including doctors and record keepers.

Nobles made up the highest social class. They were very wealthy. They often worked in the government.

Usually people stayed in the same class as their parents. But sometimes talented Egyptians rose in social rank. For instance, a skilled craftsman or a successful soldier could become quite wealthy.

Egyptian women ground grain into flour on a flat stone.
They made bread from the flour.

Egyptian children liked to wrestle,
play leapfrog, and dance.

Few women worked outside the home. Instead, they took care of their houses and families. They treated their children lovingly. Mothers often carried infants in soft slings. That way, babies could feel warm and secure.

Egypt's weather was usually hot and dry, so children spent much of their time playing outside. But they also had to work. Older children took care of younger ones. Some children also looked after their families' donkeys and goats.

Most children did not go to school. Instead, they learned what they needed to know from their parents. Mothers taught girls how to cook, weave, and raise children. Fathers taught boys how to make a living. Most boys grew up to work at the same job as their father.

Some wealthy boys went to school. There they learned reading, writing, and arithmetic. Knowing how to write was an important skill. A good writer might even grow up to work for the pharaoh.

Students practiced writing on scraps of pottery or stone.

Boys who learned to read and write could choose from many jobs as adults. They might work in a court, in the army, or in a temple.

CHAPTER TWO

Gods and Mummies

The Egyptians believed in hundreds of gods and goddesses. They kept the world in order. The Egyptians wanted to make them happy. They thought if they did, the gods would protect them.

Egyptians built many temples. Each was dedicated to a single god. A statue of this god was inside the temple. Egyptians believed it contained the god's soul.

Priests washed the statue with perfume and dressed it in clothes. They also gave it gifts of food and drink. With these gifts, they hoped to please the temple's god.

Some gods were shown with the heads of animals. For instance, in many pictures, the sun god Ra has a falcon's head.

Hathor

Ra   Osiris   Isis   Bastet   Anubis

A priest often wore a mask of the god Anubis when making a body into a mummy. Anubis was a god of the dead.

Priests were also in charge of funerals. Egyptians thought they would need their bodies after death. They found a way to preserve dead bodies. Priests turned the bodies into mummies.

To make a mummy, a priest first washed the body. He then took out some of the internal organs. The priest put the organs in special jars to protect them.

Weeks later, the priest stuffed the skin with linen or leaves. He also smeared it with sweet-smelling oil. Next, he wrapped the body in linen.

Finally, the priest read spells from the Book of the Dead. These spells protected people after death.

Egyptians loved cats. After a cat died, they sometimes mummified its body (right).

Egyptians believed in an afterlife. It was like the world we know, only better. Everyone expected to be very happy in the afterlife.

But not all Egyptians would get there. Only those who had lived good lives would be allowed in. The god Osiris decided who could enter.

After a body was made into a mummy, Egyptians placed the mummy in a tomb. This room was stocked with food, drink, clothing, jewelry, and even furniture. They believed the dead would need these things in the afterlife.

Some tombs contained small statues called shabtis (right). Egyptians believed they would turn into servants for the dead in the afterlife.

CHAPTER THREE

A Land of Builders

The Egyptian pharaohs were powerful leaders. They liked to show off their wealth by building huge structures. These structures impressed both the Egyptians and visitors to their lands.

Egyptian temples were the most important buildings in Egypt. Temples were beautiful and made of stone so they would last. No one wanted to anger a god with a poorly built temple.

One of the greatest wonders of ancient Egypt was the Great Sphinx. This giant sculpture has the head of a man and the body of a lion. Sphinxes were built to guard temples or tombs.

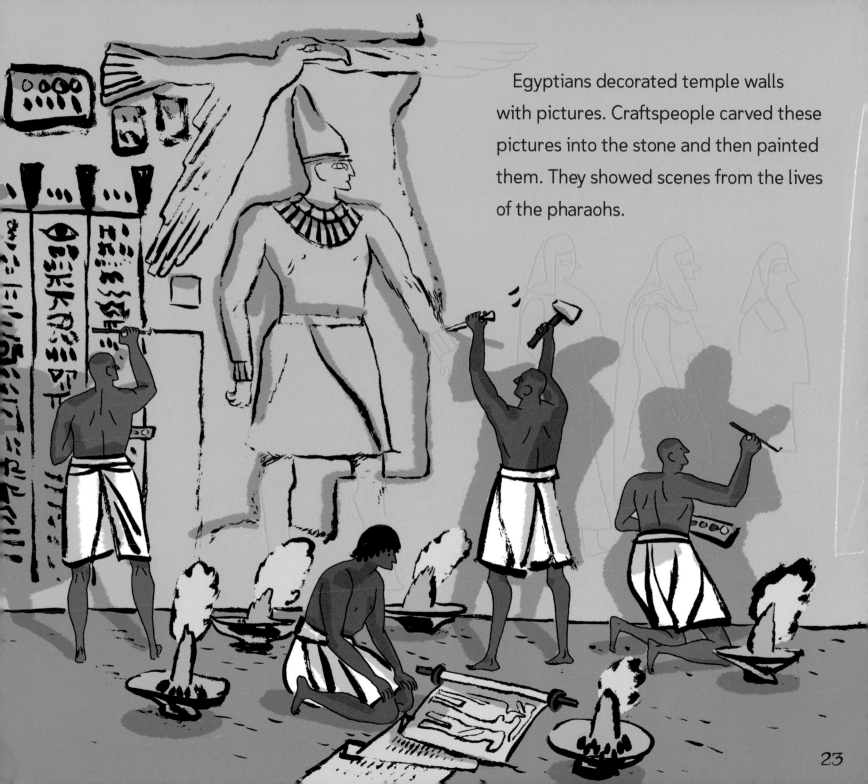

Egyptians decorated temple walls with pictures. Craftspeople carved these pictures into the stone and then painted them. They showed scenes from the lives of the pharaohs.

Just like ordinary Egyptians, the pharaohs planned for the afterlife. They prepared for their death by building huge tombs. These provided them with a comfortable life after death. The tombs also reminded people of the pharaohs' greatness. Many of the pharaohs' tombs were pyramids. Pyramids came in many sizes.

When a pharaoh died, the mummy was taken to its tomb by priests, family, friends, and servants. People carried things to place in the tomb. Some cried and threw dust on their heads to show they were sad.

In later years, pharaohs built hidden, underground tombs in a dry river valley. It is called the Valley of the Kings.

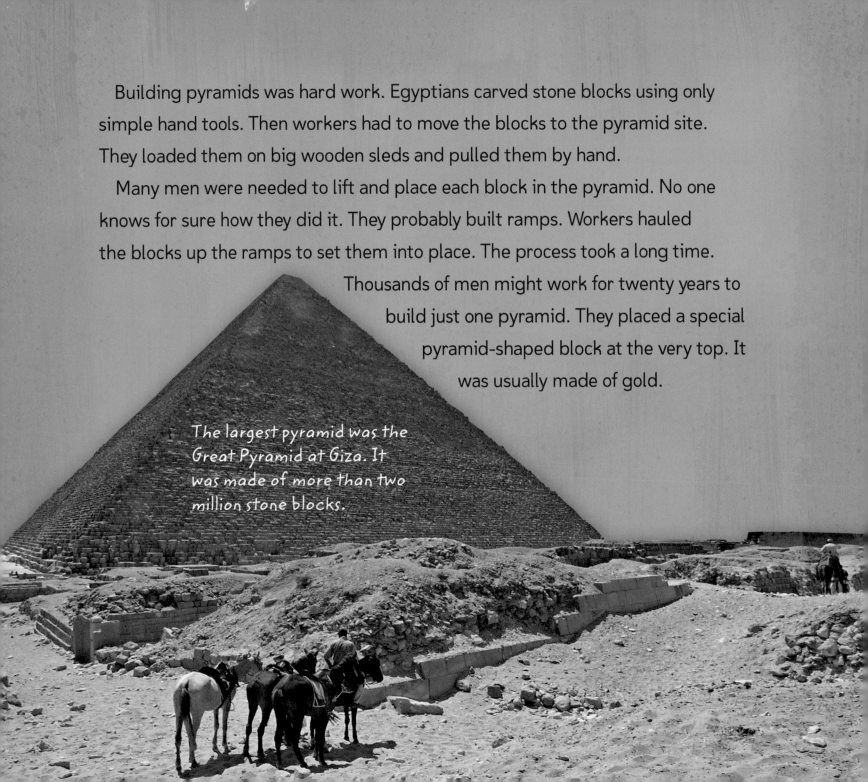

Building pyramids was hard work. Egyptians carved stone blocks using only simple hand tools. Then workers had to move the blocks to the pyramid site. They loaded them on big wooden sleds and pulled them by hand.

Many men were needed to lift and place each block in the pyramid. No one knows for sure how they did it. They probably built ramps. Workers hauled the blocks up the ramps to set them into place. The process took a long time. Thousands of men might work for twenty years to build just one pyramid. They placed a special pyramid-shaped block at the very top. It was usually made of gold.

The largest pyramid was the Great Pyramid at Giza. It was made of more than two million stone blocks.

Each block that workers lifted onto the Great Pyramid weighed about 5,000 pounds (2,270 kilograms).

27

CHAPTER FOUR

Inventions and Ideas

The ancient Egyptians depended on the Nile. They needed to bring its water to dry soil to make the land usable for farming. They came up with clever ways to do this. They built up giant piles of dirt along the river's edge. These forced the Nile to flow in new directions.

Egyptian farmers also dug ditches in the soil. The ditches helped to carry water all through a farm.

Egyptians have grown crops along the Nile for thousands of years. Low-lying farmland lines the river's edges as the Nile flows through Egypt.

Egyptians invented the shadoof to lift heavy buckets of water from the river. They used the water on farmland.

The Egyptians invented a calendar similar to our modern calendar. Like ours, it had twelve months. Months were divided into three ten-day weeks. They had several ways of telling time. At night, they guessed the hour by seeing which stars were overhead. In daylight, they told time by looking at shadows cast by the sun.

The Egyptians were expert shipbuilders. They made ships specially designed to travel the Nile.

The Egyptians were well known for their knowledge of medicine. As early as 4,500 years ago, Egyptian doctors knew how to perform some surgeries. Egyptians also knew how to make mirrors. Their mirrors were crafted from polished copper.

The Egyptians' greatest invention was papyrus. They made this type of paper from the stems of the papyrus plant.

Egyptians first soaked the papyrus stems in water. They then cut them into strips, placed them on top of one another, and pounded them together. When they dried, they made a strong sheet of paper. The Egyptians rolled these sheets into scrolls.

Papyrus was important to Egypt. On papyrus, Egyptian officials could keep written records. It helped them keep track of people and projects. Building the pyramids would have been nearly impossible without papyrus records of supplies and workers.

This papyrus scroll shows an Egyptian being judged by the god Anubis after death.

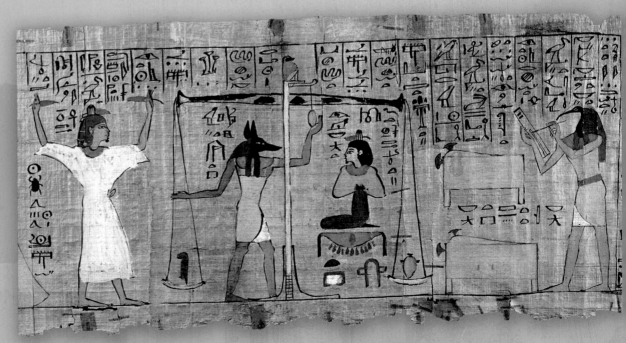

The word paper comes from "papyrus."

To keep records, the Egyptians invented a writing system. It was called hieroglyphics. Hieroglyphics included about seven hundred different signs. Some signs stood for sounds. Others stood for whole words.

People who knew how to write these signs were called scribes. Hieroglyphics was hard to learn. Scribes had to go to special schools.

Over time, people forgot how to read hieroglyphics. But in 1799, an ancient stone tablet called the Rosetta stone was discovered. It was carved with the same message in the Greek language and in hieroglyphics. Scholars who knew Greek figured out how to read hieroglyphics from the stone.

The Rosetta stone (right) is written in Greek and two styles of Egyptian writing. One style was used for religious documents or other important writing. Egyptians used the second style for more common writing.

CHAPTER FIVE

Ancient Egyptians You Should Know

Egyptian scribes used hieroglyphics to write about their times. They wrote a great deal about the pharaohs.

The army of Thutmose I invaded the land of Nubia. Nubia had lots of gold, so the invasion made Egypt richer.

Amenhotep III was a great builder. During his rule, he built temples all over Egypt.

The pharaoh Akhenaton worshipped the sun god Aten. Akhenaton claimed that Aten was the only true god. But the Egyptians liked their many gods. They continued to worship them all.

Tutankhamen is sometimes called the Boy King. He became pharaoh when he was only eight or nine.

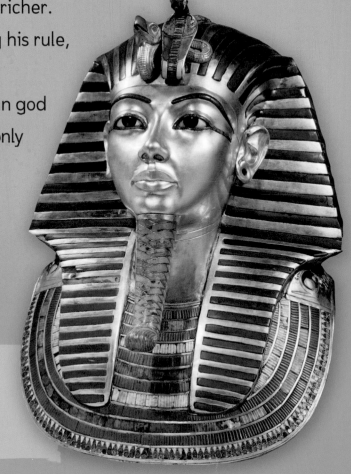

Tutankhamen's tomb housed many golden treasures, including a mask of his face.

Pharaoh Thutmose I led his army south into Nubia in the 1500s B.C. Later kings led armies northeast. They brought more land under Egypt's control.

Hatshepsut was a female pharaoh. She took power when her husband, Thutmose II, died.

Cleopatra was another woman who ruled ancient Egypt. She was famous for her intelligence and charm.

Some ordinary people were famous in ancient Egypt. Ptahhotep was a well-known writer. His book gave advice to young men. Ptahhotep said they should be kind and honest.

Imhotep was a very talented man. He designed the first pyramid. Imhotep was also famous for his knowledge of medicine. He is sometimes called the father of ancient medicine.

Pharaohs wore long fake beards with flat bottoms. Even the female pharaoh Hatshepsut wore one.

CHAPTER SIX

Egypt, Now and Then

The world of ancient Egypt lasted for thousands of years. But, in the end, foreign invaders took control of it. First, the Persians ruled Egypt. Then the Greeks did. Finally, the Romans made Egypt part of their empire in 30 B.C.

In some ways, ancient Egypt lives on. Some people devote their lives to studying its culture. They are called Egyptologists. More people study or visit Egypt for fun.

All this interest in Egypt helped create the science of archaeology. Archaeologists carefully dig ancient objects buried in the ground. Then they study the objects to learn about people from the past.

Archaeologists continue to discover ancient tombs, mummies, and objects in Egypt.

People still live along the Nile in the modern country of Egypt. Many live in large, busy cities, such as Cairo. They drive cars and work in tall buildings. In other parts of Egypt, life still has much in common with ancient times.

The ancient Egyptians influence some things we see every day. Fashion, jewelry, and even hairstyles borrow from Egyptian art.

There are even modern pyramids. In Paris, France, a glass pyramid stands outside the famous Louvre museum. It is a tribute to the ancient Egyptians and their amazing world.

Some Egyptian pyramids have crumbled over time. Piles of rubble are all we can see of these old monuments.

TIMELINE

ca. 3500 B.C.   People begin building villages along the Nile.

ca. 3100 B.C.   Pharaoh Narmer joins two separate parts of Egypt as one kingdom. Hieroglyphic writing is first used.

ca. 2650 B.C.   Architect Imhotep designs the first pyramid.

ca. 2500 B.C.   The Great Pyramid at Giza is built.

ca. 1500 B.C.   Hatshepsut begins her rule as pharaoh.

ca. 1350 B.C.   Akhenaton tries to make the Egyptians worship one god.

1323 B.C.   Tutankhamen is buried in the Valley of the Kings.

525 B.C.   Persians take over Egypt.

332 B.C.   Alexander the Great and his Greek army invade Egypt.

196 B.C.   The Rosetta stone is carved.

30 B.C.   The Romans take control of Egypt.

A.D. 1799   The Rosetta stone is discovered.

1922   Archaeologist Howard Carter discovers the tomb of Tutankhamen in the Valley of the Kings.

2007   Archaeologists confirm they have found the mummy of Hatshepsut. The pharaoh's tomb was first discovered in 1903, but the mummy was not studied until many years later.

PRONUNCIATION GUIDE

Akhenaton: AH-kuh-NAH-tuhn

Amenhotep: AH-muhn-HO-tehp

archaeology: AHR-kee-AH-luh-jee

Cleopatra: KLEE-oh-PAT-ruh

Egyptologists: EE-jip-TAH-luh-jists

Giza: GEE-zuh

Hatshepsut: hat-SHEP-soot

hieroglyphics: HY-roh-GLIF-iks

Imhotep: ihm-HO-tehp

Louvre: LOOV

Nubia: NOO-bee-uh

papyrus: puh-PY-ruhs

pharaoh: FAIR-oh

Ptahhotep: tah-HO-tehp

shadoof: shuh-DOOF

Sphinx: SFINKS

Thutmose: thoot-MOH-suh

tomb: TOOM

Tutankhamen: too-tahnk-AH-muhn

GLOSSARY

afterlife: the place where Egyptians believed they would go after they died

ancient: very old

archaeology: the study of objects left behind by ancient peoples

Egyptologist: a person who studies ancient Egypt

hieroglyphics: a form of writing used in ancient Egypt

linen: a type of cloth made from the flax plant

mummy: a dead body preserved and wrapped in linen

Nile: the great river that runs through Egypt

papyrus: Egyptian paper made from the stems of the papyrus plant

pharaoh: a ruler of ancient Egypt

pyramid: a giant structure that served as a tomb for an Egyptian pharaoh. It has four triangle-shaped sides that meet in a point at the top.

Rosetta stone: a carved stone tablet that helped modern scholars learn how to read Egyptian hieroglyphics

scribe: an Egyptian trained in writing in hieroglyphics

scroll: a document written on a long piece of paper that can be rolled up

shabti: a statue that the ancient Egyptians believed could become a servant to a dead person in the afterlife

shadoof: a simple machine that ancient Egyptians used to carry water

tomb: a structure in which a body is buried

FURTHER READING

Berger, Melvin. *Mummies of the Pharaohs*. Washington, DC: National Geographic Children's Books, 2001. Beautiful color photographs illustrate this introduction to the discovery of famous mummies.

Chrisp, Peter. *Pyramid*. New York: DK Publishing, 1998. Through large pictures and captions, this book describes each step in the building of the pyramids at Giza.

Limke, Jeff. *Isis and Osiris: To the Ends of the Earth*. Minneapolis: Graphic Universe, 2007. This graphic novel tells the ancient Egyptian story of the god Osiris and his wife, the goddess Isis. When Osiris's jealous brother Set tries to get rid of him, Isis must search far and wide to save her husband.

Stewart, David. *You Wouldn't Want to Be an Egyptian Mummy!* New York: Franklin Watts, 2000. Humorous illustrations and text describe how a mummy was made—by putting the reader in the mummy's place.

Streissguth, Tom. *Egypt*. Minneapolis: Lerner Publications Company, 2008. This photo-packed book introduces readers to the modern-day country of Egypt and its landscape, culture, people, and more.

WEBSITES

Ancient Egypt
http://www.ancientegypt.co.uk/menu.html
This site includes great information and terrific photographs from the British Museum. The "explore" sections are especially interesting.

Egyptian Galleries at the University of Pennsylvania Museum
http://www.museum.upenn.edu/new/exhibits/galleries/egyptian.html
Visit this site to find out how your name looks in hieroglyphics.

Egyptmania
http://www.clevelandart.org/kids/egypt
This website put up by the Cleveland Museum of Art has plenty of information about ancient Egypt. You can even play Senet or Hounds and Jackals, two Egyptian games.

Egypt's Golden Empire
http://www.pbs.org/empires/egypt/#
Based on a PBS television program, this site features biographies and pictures of some of the most important pharaohs.

Online Activities: Ancient Egypt
http://www.rom.on.ca/schools/egypt/activities/index.php
The Royal Ontario Museum's site includes some fun activities. You can learn how to make a mummy and write in hieroglyphics.

The Quest for Immortality: Treasures of Ancient Egypt
http://www.nga.gov/exhibitions/2002/egypt
This is a virtual exhibition produced by the National Gallery of Art. It includes photographs, slide shows, and a ten-minute video.

INDEX

PHOTO ACKNOWLEDGMENTS

The images in this book are used with the permission of: © Bill Hauser/Independent Picture Service, p. 4; © Erich Lessing/Art Resource, NY, p. 8; © Petrie Museum of Egyptian Archaeology, University College London (UC39641), p. 14; © Réunion des Musées Nationaux/Art Resource, NY, p. 19; © British Museum/Art Resource, NY, p. 20; © Travelpix Ltd./Photographer's Choice/Getty Images, p. 22; © Marwan Naamani/AFP/Getty Images, p. 26; © Roger Wood/CORBIS, p. 28; © The Bridgeman Art Library/Getty Images, pp. 32, 34; © Robert Harding World Imagery/Getty Images, p. 36; © Allan Baxter/The Image Bank/Getty Images, p. 42.

About the Illustrations

Samuel Hiti, who has a background in comic-book art, rendered the illustrations for the Life in Ancient Civilizations series using brush, ink, and computer. Hiti researched each civilization to develop distinct color palettes for these books and create his interpretations of life in these cultures.

Millbrook Press
A division of Lerner Publishing Group, Inc.
241 First Avenue North
Minneapolis, MN 55401 U.S.A.

Website address: www.lernerbooks.com

Library of Congress Cataloging-in-Publication Data

Sonneborn, Liz.
    The Egyptians : life in Ancient Egypt / by Liz Sonneborn ; illustrated by Samuel Hiti.
        p.   cm. — (Life in ancient civilizations)
    Includes index.
    ISBN: 978–0–8225–8683–8 (lib. bdg. : alk. paper)
    1. Egypt—Civilization—To 332 B.C. I. Hiti, Samuel. II. Title.
DT61.S779 2010
932—dc22   2008024716

Manufactured in the United States of America
1 2 3 4 5 6 – DP – 15 14 13 12 11 10